This is something about self-love.

OTHER BOOKS BY ROBERT M. DRAKE

Spaceship (2012)

Science (2013)

Beautiful Chaos (2014)

Black Butterfly (2015)

A Brilliant Madness (2015)

Beautiful and Damned (2016)

Broken Flowers (2016)

Seed Of Chaos (2017)

Gravity: A Novel (2017)

Moon Theory (2017)

Young & Rebellious (2018)

Chasing The Gloom (2018)

Samuel White & The Frog King (2018)

For Excerpts and Updates please follow:

Instagram.com/rmdrk
Facebook.com/rmdrk
Twitter.com/rmdrk

ISBN: 978-0-9986293-2-2

Book Cover: Robert M. Drake
Cover Image licensed by Shutter Stock Inc.

For Sevyn,

All my words are yours.
All of my words, will always be yours.

CONTENTS

MOON THEORY

ROBERT M. DRAKE

THE LUXURY

You have the luxury
of breaking
without knowing
how to heal.

And that is why you suffer
the way you suffer,

because you carry
too many pieces
and have too little time
to understand
why things hurt
the way they hurt.

THINGS FALL

The snow falls
in the winter.

The lovers fall
after midnight,
and the drinkers fall
during the long walks home.

The rain falls
in the summer.

The sun falls
to let the moon out.

And the tears
that pile over themselves
fall during war.

Things fall.
People fall.
Buildings fall.
Leaves fall.
Rain falls.

And every season,
every day,
I fall,
in many ways,

for you,

always,

for you.

EXPLAIN WHY

Sometimes
it is the things
that hurt
that save you,
and too often

those same things
bring out
both peace
and chaos,
and we cannot
explain why.

FLY LITTLE ONE

The truth is,
there is a web
of things
that do not matter,
things
that do not
feed the soul,
things
that do not
inspire the imagination,
the light.

Do not get caught in it.

Fly, little one, fly.

No matter how beautiful
the spider is,
the butterfly should always
flap its wings
a little harder
to free itself
from all
the bullshit lies.

SAD GIRL

Sad girl,
it's okay
for you to be
sad,
for sometimes

the most beautiful
people
in the world
lose everything
at the cost
of their own
hearts.

WHEN IT HAPPENS

When your heart breaks
and when your heart heals.

When someone dies
and when someone is born.

When you get a new job
and when you get fired from one.

When you succeed
and when you fail.

When you feel alone
and when your friends find you
when you need them most.

When you buy a new house
and when your car breaks down.

When you find the love
of your life,

and

when your first love hurts
your heart.

When you cry

and when you laugh.

When miracles happen
and when tragedies occur.

When life begins
and when life ends.

Trust in your timing.
Believe in your timing.

good or bad.
beer or wine.
blood or water.
peace or chaos.
heaven or hell.

We must all believe
that it is all for a purpose.

It is all part of
a grand, flawless design.

Every dot connects,
every path leads to another,
and every moment
creates another moment
to remember.

Until our bones dry
and our memories rise

toward the sun.

We must,
at all times,
always,
gracefully welcome
all the things
we are meant for.

WHAT WE CAUSE

And now,

after everything
you've been through,

here you are,
among the gods,

laughing
and drinking
despite all of
the pain
the world might
have caused.

WHAT YOU ARE NOT

You are not soft.

You are not breaking
and
you are not fragile,
despite
what the world
has told you.

You are not weak.

You are not dumb
and you are certainly
not falling.

You are not made
of inconsistencies,
theories, or incomplete
sentences.

No, none of that.
Please throw that madness
out the window.

You are a goddamn soldier
in the middle of a war.

You are the goddamn

split second between
life and death.

Between what is certain
and what might never become.

You are the shooting star
that suddenly flashes in
the night sky.

You are all
the goddamn trees
in the world,
all the oceans,
and all the fires,
in one human.

You are what is left.

You are your ancestors'
legacy, their dreams, and
their aspirations.

You are the motionless rock
in a river full of lies.

You are.

You are.

You are.

Make your life count.

Fuel the fire,

and burn,
and be,
and become,
and do

all the things for which
you were meant for.

BE PROUD

There is
nothing
to be proud
of
when you have
outgrown
what hurts.

That only means
you have forgotten
how to feel,
and sometimes

there is
nothing
worse
than that.

THE TRUTH HURTS

But it is true

that the deepest oceans
are the quietest,
and the deepest wounds
are the same.

And the people
around you
are the only ones
who can hear both.

Sometimes,
your friends
know you better
than you think,
and sometimes

they feel what you feel
by listening
to the loudest roars
in the room:

your pain,
your silence.

Appreciate them,
for when you believe that

no one is there,

and that you are alone,

they are there,
and believe
that they understand
how you feel.

HOW MANY TIMES

Here is
one thing
I have learned
about people:

the human heart
forgives

and forgives

and forgives,

no matter
how many times
it has been
broken.

PRESS ITSELF

I want you
to discover yourself again,

to find what matters,
what hurts,
and I want you
to be proud of what you've accomplished.

I want you to feel
no regret,

to cure yourself
from self-doubt,
and I want you to remember
all the pain
everyone has caused…

so that you don't
carelessly press it against
someone else.

I want love to find you,
but not just any kind of love.

For you,
I want the kind that will
keep you up at night,

the kind that makes the world
stop at your feet,
and the kind that takes
your breath away
when you remember to breathe.

I want so many things for you
that I don't care about myself.

I just want to see you
fucking happy,
because I know

that somewhere
in that beautiful heart of yours,

there is a light
trapped within,

a certain kind of miracle,

a delicate genius
that drives you,
that makes you.

And it should be free,
born out of the wild,

and built from the atoms of trust,
peace,
and freedom.

So please
find it in you
to find yourself again.

Find the courage
to find your better days,
and never lose track
of the laughter
that's meant to find you.

After all,
you are all things
that inspire the fire,

all things
that bring people closer together,

and all things
most people cannot understand.

SECOND CHANCE

And yes,

you do deserve
someone
who loves you,
but what you deserve
most
is happiness.

Whether you are alone
or not.

You deserve
to know your smile

when no one
is around.

BEAUTIFUL DEAR

My dear,

I hope you understand,
that all the men
who have ever called you
beautiful
and have left you
with a broken heart

are full of shit, and yes,

most of them have said
anything to have you
for the night.

But of all the flames that riot
out of their mouths,
understand,
that one thing is true.

Understand
that you *are, indeed,* beautiful,
my dear, and
you have always been.

It is just that
you have had a streak
of distasteful love,

love that does not
make this hard life any kinder.

And understand,
that it is not you.

And believe
that there is nothing wrong
with your heart,
with your soft love.

It is just,
most men do not appreciate
what they have
until it is too late,
and believe
that it will
always be *too late*.

But that is how life is, right?
Correct?

You can never have
what you want at the right time.
You could never
be too ready
for all the hurting that comes
your way.

Yes, my dear,

life is one hot ball of flame,
and men,
well,
most of them are undeserving
but not all of them.

Some of them
are just as gentle
and delicate as you are.

Some of them have fought
the good fight
and can tell the difference
between a scar
and a bruise.

Some of them understand
and some of them
have loved hard enough
to know a flower
when they see one.

So, not all are terrible.

My dear, understand,
that the right man
for you is out there
and that he might not be
perfect but he will be good enough
and understand

that he will bloom with you
and the world will take notice
of this connection.

And together the two of you
will give humanity
the faith it needs
to believe in love again.

To believe in its search
and the confidence to know
that true love
is out here for everyone,
that is,

to those who hold patience
on the tips of their fingers.

Understand this, my dear.

Understand that yes,
all men are created equal,
but it takes more than
just a man to love a woman.

Understand, that it takes guts.

Understand that your heart
is worth a thousand years,
and only a man with love
on his hands is worth your time.

PEOPLE HURT

And some people hurt
and sometimes

those same people
don't tell anyone
about it.

They just watch
their world crumble,
without anyone
there to notice

how they fall.

HOW FAR IT GOES

And then you asked

why I was so obsessed with pain,

and why it hurt the way it hurt.

And it was simple ...

Because your body is made
of flesh and bones.

Because your tears come
from the soul.

Because your heart does more
than just keep you alive.

Because sometimes your thoughts
are your worst enemy.

Because you want someone
to hold you,
but the people you know
aren't strong enough.

Because no matter how far you go,
there is always something
taking you back.

Because certain songs represent you.

Because you want to change people's lives,
but you don't know how
or where to begin.

Because sometimes
other people's art makes you cry.

Because. Because. Because.

And you will search for reasons why,
and you will never find them.

Because things hurt,
they are supposed to.

As long as you care,
something will always hurt.

So take that with you,

take it toward the darkness,
toward the light ...

and please,
never stop caring.

Know that pain
is just another product,
another synonym

for all the things
you love.

WHAT TO THINK

You think this is your life.

That waking up every day,
working the same job
for years is enough.

That listening to the same songs,
thinking of the same movies
is all there is.

That telling yourself "tomorrow"
instead of "today"
is what keeps you alive.

You think this is living?
What breath should consist of?

That perhaps,
deep within the wells of your heart,
you believe that you
do not deserve better?

The human heart is
the devourer of doubt.

And that is something we
do not understand.

But

I want to tell you something
no one has ever told me.

I want to tell you
that there is inspiration everywhere.

That there is fire in the coldest
of places, and that
light is born of darkness.

I want to tell you
that when you are sad,
laughter is soon to follow.

And when all is lost,
there is always hope
lurking in the background.

Believe it.

Now, of course,

I'm not trying to preach,
because I am no preacher,
but you have got to
find it in you to live.

To figure things out.

To make mistakes
and break your own heart,
over and over.

To escape this reality
to which you've been born in.

Because there is more,
a lot more, and there will
always be more.

Believe it.

And I am not saying
to go out and do one thing.

No, what I'm saying is,
to go out and do many things,
things of which you're afraid of.

Things that are worth
staying up all night for.

Things that will make you
see the magic.

I want you to fall
for the rest of your life,
but I also want you to rise
every time you touch the ground.

To rise stronger, wiser, and kinder.

Because in the end,

it is true,

we are all birds
flying against the wind.

And we are all
in search of a place,
in search of others,
and in search of all
the little things that
remind us of home.

Just believe it,

and know that you
deserve more.

IF THEY WANT

If they want you,

they will not lose you
and that is how it works.

If someone loves you,
they will take the sky

if you cannot fly

And if you cannot swim,

they will drink the ocean
to make sure
you do not drown.

TELL HER

And then,
a girl writes to me.

And she asks me what do to,
because her boyfriend
cheats on her.

And I tell her what to do.

I tell her to leave the city,
to leave him behind.

To forget about people like him,
that he is too dangerous
to keep around.

To burn the memory of him
and delete everything that
pulls her in.

To defeat the gravity,
the magnitude that tears bring.

But, of course,
she already knew this.

But, of course,
she knows right from wrong.

But, of course,
she knows she deserves better.

But the truth is,
I know she will do
the exact opposite.

Because this is something
we have all
learned the hard way.

And we all know that

the human heart
forgives
and forgives
and will *ALWAYS* forgive…

no matter
how many times
it has been broken.

The heart accepts
what it desires,
no matter how closed
its doors are.

READING POEMS

I'm tired of reading
love poems.

I'm tired of listening
to love songs.

I'm tired of watching
the same movies
with the same actors
who play the same roles
and dive into the same plots.

Hell, this kind of thinking
makes it okay for me
to run around in circles.

To live the same life
over and over.

To fall into the same love
in order to feel the same pain
and to experience
the same things
over and over again.

But I want change. I demand it.

I want to wake up one day

in a completely different city
without knowing
what I'm going to do,

who I'm going to talk to,
or how my day is going to end.

Imagine that.

I want to meet
a different person every day
and I want to learn
something new
as they come and go.

I want love
but not the kind we know,
not the kind we are meant
to believe we deserve.

I want more. I deserve more.

I know it!

I want the kind
that keeps me on my toes
and keeps me dancing drunk
on the edge without worrying
if I fall or if I fly.

The kind that is hard

but worth my time.

And the kind I could
hold on to during the nights
I feel most alone.

You know,
the kind that people say
is not real
but somewhere down the line
you discover it for yourself,

that kind.

And I don't want the kind
that breaks me
the moment they leave,

not the kind that is exploited
throughout the media:

through sex and beauty,
through chaos and pain.

No,
that love doesn't represent me, us.

For there is no glory in heartache.

There is no light in pain.

No shelter in tears
and no comfort in sadness.

I don't want anything
to do with that.

I don't want their
manufactured love.

I don't believe in it.

I don't want
what they talk about,
what they represent,
what they sell.

I can't afford it.

Give me what is real,
what grants life,
what heals
the deepest wounds.

That is what I need,
what we all need.

And I hope that one day
we find it.

I hope that one day
we find our humanity

and learn to love one another
for what we truly are.

I hope that one day
we find what is missing

because

I know we are capable
of so much more.

HARD TO FORGET

It's hard to forget
when the ocean
can't wash away scars.

While sometimes
the waves crashing
bring memories
toward the shore.

And I miss you.

I miss you in the water,
laughing,
smiling,
bringing peace to
the madness
of my days.

You see,
within you,
you carried this
certain kind of paradise.

A delicate wind.

A delicious ocean
on a hot summer day,

and I want you.

I want the way your hair
tangles on my fingertips
while we're lying
beneath the sun,

soaking in the rhythm
of broken love.

And I say it is broken,
because from the start
we knew how it would
eventually fall apart.

As all good things do,
as all bright fireballs fade.

You see, kid,
we were like two suns
too close to each other.

Two suns fighting
to see which one would
outshine the other.

And yeah,
we got too close,
but that's the point, right?

We're supposed to clash,

ride, and burn.

We're supposed to have fallouts
and rise above the chaos of love,
the lie of love.

But that's the promise,
isn't it?

Like one moment
we feel unstoppable
and then, in a blink of an eye,
it all just goes to shit,
to vapor.

It suddenly vanishes before us
like the liquor that drips
off the glass.

But that's the cycle,

to feel invincible,
to slowly die …
this heroic death
as all brave people do.

That's what the promise is.

How nothing beautiful
is meant to last forever
but long enough

to really fuck you over,

to really change your heart,
your life's direction,
and make the moments
we shared hard to forget.

I miss you, kid. I really do.

And sometimes I think about you
and this is what happens when I do.

I lose control.
I go mad.
I write what hurts.
I swim into the darkness
of my own soul
and drown.

And no matter how much
you prepare yourself for
the end of things,
for the way the heart breaks,

the way the soul cracks,
the shattering of thoughts,
and the clattering of bones,

you never know how you're
going to take it in,

until it comes rioting down.

For sometimes
the love of your life
is meant to destroy you
and all you can do is
watch

as everything you've known
goes to hell.

TRAVEL FAR

Things go as far
as you let them go.

So if you let people in,
it is only because you
opened the door.

If you let people love you,
it is only because you
let them into your heart,
and if you let people break you,

it is only because you
gave them the right
to drop you at any given time
at all.

So what we have here, darling,
is the power of perspective.

And people will always do
what they must to get by,
but how they affect you
is the difference, your choice,
and sometimes that
is the most important
choice of them all.

WAKING MORNING

When you wake up,
who are you?

Who do you think
you are throughout the day,
during the night,
and when you are asleep?

Tell me, do you know?

Are you someone
who is looking for a beginning?

Someone who is looking
for a place to bear all of their pain?

Are you that person
swimming up the stream,
fighting the current of what is
and what shall never be?

Are you that dreamer,
that thinker,
that lover?

Or are you the one who
watches the falling stars
as they pass above the window?

Are you the nine-to-fiver
with no hope? who
wants more but doesn't know
how to find it? who doesn't
know if the pursuit of happiness
is worth pursuing?

Who are you, sweet darling,
tell me, who?

Are you the kind of person
who is isolated in the morning
but loving and kind
and tender and gentle at night?

Are you someone who feels more
than other people or
someone who feels disconnected
from it all?

Are you the one who sheds
a handful of tears when no one
is around?

Are you alone?
Are you in good company?
Are you the fallen?
The hurt?
The beaten?
The lost?
The confused?

Are you the hidden poem
in a forgotten book?

Or that one beautiful moment
that is ignored?

Tell me, you beautiful human,
who do you think you are?
And when you wake up,
tell me, how does that
heart feel?

What does it feel?

Do you feel as if the world
is in the palm of your hands?

Do you feel the inspiration
flowing within you?

The blooming of all that you are?

Or

do you feel broken?

Shattered, soft and fragile?

Do you feel like you have lost
your way?

Tell me, what do you know
about yourself?

What have you learned
through the years?

Have you learned about
people? about togetherness?
about friendship and loyalty?

Have you learned about
what gets you ticking?

What gets you drunk?
What sends you over the edge,
to fly toward all the people
you need and love?

Tell me if your arms are wide open
or if your eyes are closed shut.

Tell me how you kiss.

How you hold sadness
in your body, but don't pour it
onto the world.

Tell me why you talk the way you talk
and say precious words
when you look at the mirror.

Tell me, do you love yourself?
but do you really love yourself?
and feel it deep within your bones?

Tell me what you will do
if the world ends and who
you will save.

Will you save yourself?

Tell me, who are you?
Who are you in the morning
and who are you in the evening?

A lover?
Or are you one of the sad people?

And tell me if you are happy
with whomever you have chosen
to become.

I've got all night to hear
your story.

DESTROY YOU

Whatever you do
do not let the things
you love destroy you.

Because you
never get back
that piece of yourself
you lost

and knowing this
bit of information,

knowing how it ends,
we still let the things
we love devour us.

We make love to the,
and feel disconnected because of them.

What great practically,
to lose your heart,
mind,
and soul as the cost
of love.

KEEP GOING

You've got to keep going
even if it kills you.

Hang on to the light
even if it is you who
causes it to fade away,
You've got to walk toward life
and grab it
like the spider
when it finds its prey.

You've got to love all the time
and realize that no matter
how mad it gets to live,

kindness
is the best practice.

You've got to undo what you've done,
unlearn what you've learned,
and begin all over again.

You've got to gracefully
say the right words
and the wrong ones,
during both good and bad times.

You've got to go

even if you don't know
where it is you're going.

You've got to lose everything,
let go of all possessions,
and discover
that everything you have
ever had to offer
has always been within you.

You've got to climb
toward the top of the mountain
and realize
that you shouldn't stop there,

and that the strength to do so
will not come from the body
but from the heart.

You've got to understand
that it is all in the heart,
that it begins and ends
in the heart, and that only
the heart can either destroy you
or grant you a second chance
at love, at life.

You've got to trust
how things happen,
trust miracles and tragedies,
and remember how they both

arrive unexpected.

You've got to live,
really live
from the marrow of your bones
until you've got everything
behind you and
you have nothing left to feel.

You've got to find
the inspiration to walk out
of your shell, to break out of it,

to know your boundaries
and conquer them,
to define new limits,
to defeat them again.

Over and over
till the heart can no
longer go on.

You've got to do these things,
try these things,
and do something,

because if not,
nothing happens
and nothing
ever will.

PEOPLE TROUBLE

I like people
who've been through trouble.

Who've seen things,
felt things most haven't.

They're like old books,
books with torn covers,
with missing pages.
They've been through
several different hands
before they've reached your own.

I appreciate a good book like this.

Good company like this.

A one on one,
day in and day out.

People and books are the same,
for the two are seeds
from the same flower.

The two age gracefully
and are best
when you experience
them alone.

But never mix the two,
for sometimes a brilliant book
is written by a shitty person,
and sometimes a good person
writes a shitty book.

The two do not always go
hand in hand.

Nonetheless,

both should be well lived,

well loved,
and well experienced.

With tenderness,
kindness, and care,

Take this with you:

now, good night,
motherfucker

and read: both people and books
at different moments

and at

different times.

IT IS IN YOU

The chaos is you.

The noise
and the cold chills
and the swaying of time
dwell within you.

This is what it is like
when someone dies.

This is what it is like
when your heart breaks.

This is what it is like
when letting go
is your only option.

The body becomes numb,
the mind becomes a feather,
and the longing to be held
becomes the wind.

Your insecurities are demons
and your heart is a cathedral
on fire.

You burn.

You burn in the morning.
You burn in the afternoon.
You burn in the evening.

You burn,
and you do so—bright enough
to light the midnight sky.

This is what it is like
when you are lost.

This is what it is like
when you have gone mad,
when you have seen too much
of what is not really there.

People keep asking you
what is wrong and you keep
telling them, but no one
around you understands.

No one around you connects
the possibility,
and no one seems to care enough
to unfold the dealings
of your mind.

The chaos is you;
it is not around you.
Pay attention.

The buildings are collapsing.

The oceans are drying
and you barely trust
yourself in your own skin.

The chaos is born of you,
it is you, and it is not
always a bad thing.

You are the lion among the hyenas.
The diamond beneath the mountain.
The gold in the middle of the ground.
The eye of the storm.
The rarity of love.

Listen to the walls
as they fall, as they crumble.

Listen to the way
the rain hits the window.

Listen to the waves
and to the sound the sparks
make as they greet the air.

They are talking within you
and they are all
whispering the same thing
at the same time:

"The power is in you."

"The power is in you."

"The power is in you."

The past increases
and so does the chaos

if you do not see the future
ahead.

As the noise
and the cold chills
and the swaying of time
continue to move
within you.

The power is you,

so take it
and make everything
you have ever wished for
yours.

EVERYTHING SAD

Everything is sad.

I almost feel sorry for everyone
regardless of how good they have it,
how bad it all goes.

There's just something in people's eyes that
makes me feel sad.

I look at their fingernails.
I look at their hair,
the way they speak, and the way
their clothes hang from their bodies.

And sometimes I cry.

The days have gone by
when the mad,
the crooked,
and the shady
all have my condolences.

Either that or
maybe I am a bit too emotional
lately.

I blame my daughter.
She has changed me.

She has made me feel more
than I usually do.

I want to save everyone.

My heart is finally open.
My heart is finally free.

And I blame a little girl for this.

She has taught me more
about myself than I could have.

And now,
too often,
when I think of how people
fall in love or how people
sing while everyone is watching,

I think of her,

and then I believe how easy it is
to do so—
when the right person
presents themselves

to show you how
you have had it all wrong
this long.

SHATTER ALONE

Often do I think about
the last time my soul shattered
and how I felt alone.

And too often
do I think about
the last time I was happy
and I, too, felt alone.

Does it ever make a difference?
Is it supposed to tear you apart?

That is, knowing how impossible
it is to feel the same things.

I think, yes,
we are meant to live
with other people,
share our lives
with other people,
but the reality is that
we experience
what we experience on our own.

We could be together,
laughing, drinking,
having a good time,
but my experience could be

different from yours.

Well, of course,
our realities are
a thousand miles apart,
perhaps even galaxies
apart.

But that is what has a hold of me.

That is what has me washed
up on the shore, gasping for
air that doesn't even exist.

The fact
that I will never know
what she was feeling,

thinking, while we were together:
laughing, drinking,
and those precious soft
moments we exchanged love.

And now the clock
whispers and reminds me
of how rapidly I have become
less of who I was
and more of someone
I do not recognize.

But what is the difference, right?

If we shared a moment,
does it mean we were happy?
Or does it mean I thought
we were doing so well
that it eventually
turned to shit?

Or

even worse,
did I know the real you?
did you know the real me?

Or did I fall in love
with someone I created
in my head,
someone I thought I knew?

The dark inspiration flows
while I stay in my bedroom
thinking of all the reasons
why I could have done more,

been myself, you know?

But I am alone
as you are alone.

We are empty spaces
full of land

and every so often
do we come to visit
the graves we dug
on our own.

The past hurts, it stings
and memories are ghosts,
ones that haunt the livening

and ones that wished

they could have lived
a little more.

MAD DOGS

My friends,

I have seen the dogs,
the mad ones,
the ones who are starved
of love.

And the ones who want
what I have.

I tell 'em
they can have it,
all of it,
to the last drop.

I give them this,
and that.

I give them my gold,
my house, my money.

I give them my success,
my cars, and my shoes.

They can have it all.
I don't need it.

Load the truck

and take everything with you,
but for Christ's sake
do not take the poetry.

Do not strip me of my art
of my heart, my soul.

That belongs to the people.

It belongs on the street
for all who are listening—
begging to hear.

You can take everything
from a man,
but please,

don't take his spirit.

Once you do,
he pretty much has
nothing else to live for.

Amen.

SKULL JUMPS

The thoughts of you
remain in the skull

and the liquor
remains in the blood.

The moon dives
as the sun jumps.

The switch is continuous.

And then
the next day arrives

and I ask myself,

*What is the difference
between the two?*

And there is none,

for both are things
I still haven't learned
to recover from,

and both are things
that still have me

right where they want me.

Sadness conquers while liquor
is poured, and I fall on the pavement

when I mix the two.

The end.

YOU TAKE IT IN

Isn't it sad,
that you might never be
who you were meant to be?

Perhaps, but here is something
to dwell on, to think about.

Everything you need
is not what you need.

You see,
the thing is,
everything you take in
is part of a great scheme,
a manufacturing of love,
of need, of want.

And you wake up like this,
believing that you are not
beautiful.

That you are not worthy
of your skin,
mind, and heart.

But it is not your fault.

Can you imagine the kind

of social programming
you have been given
since birth? forced, since birth.

The brain washing.

The endless hours
and hours of
being told what to do
subconsciously, so
that you do not even notice
you are being controlled,
directed
into what to think,
feel, and or even love.

This is not freedom.
Freedom is absolute isolation.

But isolation is death.

Isolation is madness
and if not at first,
then eventually it will be.

The corporations
have stripped our confidence,
our imaginations and dreams.

We are no longer human.
We can no longer dream.

We can no longer sleep.
We are no longer safe.

And we are no longer spiritual beings
capable of growing our own love.

This, we do not see.
Our eyes have been removed.

We love what we *think* we love,
what we think we *need*.

We believe what they
want us to believe.

Confusion is the barrier.

But what can we do?
How can we break free
of this unforgiving chain
of control?

The epiphanies are everywhere,
even where you least
expect them to be.

They could be in your house.
In your mother's eyes.
At the bus stop or even
in the middle of the street,
waiting to be found. And that is it.

That feeling you get
when something feels right
but your mind tells you
to think twice.
That's what's real.

That is who you are,
what you are *really*
thinking you need, want.

That's your soul talking,
your heart going against
the grain.

Follow that intuition,
know it,
and make it yours.

That is your exit.
That is your magnificent truth.

And that is what is extraordinary
about being human.

The ability to snap out
of the bullshit
and realize what is important,
and the ability to realize
what is not.

You have it in you.

You have that power.

Know it

and

become who you
were meant to become
and avoid what you are
told to feel

at
all
cost.

A DARLING MEMORY

A few years ago,
I met a darling
named Samantha.

She was almost too
perfect to bear.

She was fresh,
like new words
to a writer.

Strong, bold, smart,
and clever.

She was a goddess, with
her curly hair that dangled
down her back
and dragged the ocean
as she walked.

Either way, I ruined it.
It didn't go as planned.

Well, that and,
of course, she had a flaw.

Her tongue and attitude
were sharper than knives.

She would complain
over and over
and beef about
how I did not return her calls
how I forgot sometimes
to text her back
and how we did not
go out enough.

I did not understand it.
I gave her what I had
or whatever it was I had left.

Or maybe I did understand it
and I did not have it in me.

Or maybe

I was too fucking busy
to be friends, let alone lovers.

I did not have the time.

I never do.

JUST ANOTHER WAY

And there are
a million ways
to tell you
how it feels,

but you will never
understand it.

Because
I never stopped
loving you,

and loving you

is just another way
of telling you
how hard it is
to let you
go.

LETTING GO

Baby, I know you think
I'm like the rest,
but I'm not like most.

And I get it, I really understand.

I know how hard it is
to be told to hold on
when there's nothing left
to hold on to.

I know how sometimes
change means growing
apart from best friends.

And I know how letting go
can mean several
different things.

Like waiting for someone
who is never meant to arrive,
and telling yourself to wait
a little longer.

So damn, yeah, I get it.
Believe me, I do.

I know you want to love

but you don't know
what love is,
and I know you want
to be yourself
and stop apologizing
for who you are.

It is just
that things move you,
things make you feel
a certain way.

I know you're looking
for good people,
for good hands to hold on to.

So yeah, I get it.

You're the last of your kind.
But you're not,
because I'm here with you,
surviving,
defeating the odds,
and I am telling you
that you're not alone.

That you've never been
and that you never have to be.

It is just that

people like us want
to feel something,
a moment
that is meant to give us
life forever.

And that's why I get it,
because I see myself in you
and we belong together.

It is true.

Anything else wouldn't

make much sense at all.

BROKEN THINGS

At some point,

you've got to realize
when it's time
for yourself,
when it's time
to heal.

You've got to look
at your hands

and know
that they are capable
of mending all kinds

of broken things.

SWEET GIRL

My sweet girl,
if I am ever missing,
if I am gone in another world,

please remember this.

Please remember
to remind yourself
of this.

Remember that not
all people are bad,
that not all people are good.

That everyone has both
light and darkness, and it is
up to you to seek the light,
and I hope you
always choose the light.

Remember
that sometimes
people actually want to help you,
but also remember
that sometimes
people want to use you
for their gain.

Remember that everything
you do is a shot in the dark,
regardless of how prepared
you might think you are.

And because of that,
know that you'll never
be prepared enough,
and that everything that
is meant to happen—will happen.

And that when they happen,
it will be out of your reach,
out of your control
but how they affect you
will always be on *you*.

Remember that you will
never quite understand other people,
let alone yourself.

That you will commit
more mistakes than certainty.

Remember that things will
get bad, really bad, and that's inevitable,
but also remember that not
all storms last forever.

Remember how nothing
is ever yours, that everything

has an expiration date,
from memories, to things,
to people and places.
Nothing ever lasts,
so please take letting go lightly
and kindly.

My sweet girl, I can only
hope that I am there for you
to remind you of all these things.

Now, I am sure that I am missing
a few things here and there.

But ultimately,
if there is one thing to remember,
then let it be this:

That drinking wine
is good for the soul.

That good company
really is good company.

That failure is a beautiful thing.

And that you don't have to prove yourself to
anyone other than yourself.

Oh, my sweet girl,
the thing is,

you can't trust anyone,
and sometimes
not even yourself.

Life is hard, confusing,
and strange.

Remember that,
always.

STARS IN FRONT OF ME

The other day was a hot day
and I was stuck in traffic
going south.

The man in front of me starts
beeping, bickering about
the cars not moving.

Now, I understand him,
because a hot day
and traffic don't mix,
they don't see
eye to eye with each other.

Soon after, the cars in front of us
begin to move, and out
of nowhere comes another
car and cuts the guy off.

He bickers some more
and flips the guy off.

Soon enough
we are all back where we were:
in the middle of traffic,
dreaming of rivers,
wind currents,
and all things that flow.

Moments later the two start
insulting each other, and it got
to the point where the two brawled
all over the street over nothing.

The nerve of these people.
Now the traffic is worse
than what it was.

And then they go home, as if
nothing is wrong
and they don't see the issue.

They never do.

But I do.

The problem with these kind
of people is,
that they have never
seen death.
They have just
read about it in the paper.

They have never been defeated.
They have just
heard about it
over the radio.
And they have never
felt love.

They have just seen it
on TV.

Otherwise,

not much
would bother them,

if they did.

THE HOLY WORD

The holy word is,
do not expect much of people.

Do not put your faith in humanity.

If you have to put your trust,
your life,
between a man
and a dog,

then by all means,
choose the dog.

Most men do not know
what to do with their lives,
let alone with the trust
of other people.

A dog
will look you in the eyes
with sincerity and bark
before its teeth pierce your skin,

whereas a man
will stab a knife
into your back and smile,

and you will never see it

coming.

Most never do,

because most men
are cowards.
And dogs?
Well, dogs are dogs,
and men are men
in all their glory.

And the difference is a tragedy.
Both are capable of love,
but only one gives it

and expects nothing in
return.

BIRDS CHIRPING

And now,
you have found
your way back
into my life again.

And the birds
do not chirp the same.

The clouds do not shift the same.
The oceans do not sway the same.

Things change.
People change.
Places change.

The universe
and its stars change.

And now
the flowers have bloomed
within the marrow
of my bones
despite
what you've picked,
cut,
or burned to the ground.

Things have changed

but I'm still me.

I'm still the same garden
you forgot to water.

I'm still the same
soul without a body.

I'm still a half-empty
bottle of whiskey
and a mind full
of forbidden thoughts.

But what a blessing
it is to survive.

For now,
I'm all things that grow
in the darkness
and without you,

I am.

I am.

I am.

And I am more me
than I have ever been.

Amen.

DESERVE THE WORLD

Just because
you love them,
it doesn't give them
the right to hurt you.

Protect yourself,
love yourself,

no matter who's
breaking you apart.

You deserve the world
and I hope

it doesn't take
a lifetime to realize

that.

DELICATE FLOWERS

She is all things
that are delicate.

All things soft.
All things gentle.
All things that
soar low above
the quiet sea.

She is all time
that heals.

Every second
when a petal falls.

Every minute
when a leaf sweeps
across the floor.

She is all reason
to give all soul.

And all reason
to give all hours.

She makes me betray myself,
lose all of my motors skills
and float toward

her like a fallen feather

landing on her cheek.

I am sincerely hers.

This damned body of mine.
This damned mind of mine.
This damned heart of mine.

All, sincerely hers.

I wear her love, and
it shelters the chaos,
the madness—the shooting of stars.

She soothes the ache of
the soul, the craving
of friendship and
the missing of good company.

Without her,
I am not interested in art.

In words that mend
the brokenness, that is
the youth.

It is hard,
and I understand that
not everyone will

love me,
that not everyone
is going to trust me.

But her,

I am sincerely hers,

and it doesn't take
a genius to realize this.

She grants me peace.

She is mother of all that flows
and she corrects

every mistake,
question,
and endeavor

I have ever had
about the
longing of sweet love.

LOVE AGAIN

We all know
it is important to fall,
shatter, and cry.

Life has to be
perfectly balanced,
but you know
what's more important
than falling apart?

The way you put yourself
back together.

The way you learn
what you have unlearned,
and the way you get
right back up

to love again.

ON ANOTHER PLANET

Maybe on another planet
there are two people
who dress like us,
talk like us,
and laugh like us.

And maybe right now,
in this very moment,
those same two people
are looking at the sky,

pointing at the stars,
wondering
if there are two people
like them,
somewhere,

in the vastness of the universe.

And maybe
they feel the same things
we feel,
despite how different
their planet might be.

Ironic enough, right?

Imagine that,

you and I,
together in all worlds,
an infinite chain of love.

That is what I want for us.

I want to love you
in all places,
in all times,
and a thousand years from now.

That is the only dream
I see us living.

WORDS ARE WORDS

Because words are words
and actions are actions
and the two don't mix.

So if you say
that you love me,
then show me
without reason.

Show me with care
and softness.

Make me know
that I am irreplaceable.

That I am the only person
who matters.

MISTAKES DONE

What is done
is done
and you must learn
from your past
and you must know
that your mistakes
are more
than just mistakes.

You must know
that they are lessons.

And sometimes
they'll break you,
and at other times
they'll reveal everything,

including

who you really are.

IT HURTS

It hurts
because pain alters
everything.

It either brings you
closer together
or makes you drift
farther apart.

It either destroys you
or makes you stronger.

Know the difference.

Not all pain is bad, so
welcome it
and know that sometimes
tears can
cleanse the soul.

BEFORE I GO

Before I go,

just promise
that you'll hold on

to yourself

when life gives you
every reason
to fall apart.

I FEEL YOU

So,
just because
we have different
lives
doesn't mean
I don't know
what it's like.

Pain is relative.

If you cry,
I cry.

If you feel,
I feel.

My scars are your scars,
and they are both born
of the same
fire.

SILENT DREAMS

I hear you,
because sometimes

the sound
of your soul
is the most beautiful

thing in the world.

EXPECT TO BREAK

And the breaking
of one's heart
never feels
how you'd expect it
to feel.

And after the last good-bye,
you're never quite
the same.

And as the years pass,
it becomes harder
to find love.

And some days
you feel everything,
the deepest wounds
on fire.

And the words,
"Don't leave"
cling to the tip of your tongue.

And if it hurts,
it's because you still care.

And the world keeps
going, but everything

within reach is completely
still.

This is what the end
feels like.

Like memories fading
into the darkness
as you watch my sadness devour
my skin.

And as I stand before
your ghost,

I am,

and I am blooming
into something beautiful,
something

I know you will never
have the chance
to see,
to feel,

and to love.

HARD SCARS

Sometimes,

the strongest
hearts
have
been dropped
the hardest

and sometimes,

the strongest
people
have
the most scars.

REASON TO LIVE

You're brave,

because life gives
you
every reason
to want to give up
and still,

you rise.

You pick yourself up
and carry on.

THE RULES OF

Here are
the rules of endearment:

Make your own path,
your own rules.

Be your own king
or queen.
Don't let anyone
tell you
how to live,
when to breathe,
or what to love.

Believe in something.
Hold on to it
and try not to
let it go.

Take care of yourself,
trust a handful of people
and always follow
your heart.

Find the good word,
the good food,
and the good music,

and live by them.

Make sure every moment counts,
and above all,
be kind,

for kindness is the greatest
perk in life.

It can take you anywhere.

It can send you to the moon
without ever
leaving the ground,

and it can save lives
in the blink
of an eye.

UNDERSTAND ME

You don't have to
close yourself up

because there will

always be someone
who understands
what it's like

to keep your heart open

while it's breaking
apart.

WE SHARED THAT

Everyone
has lost
someone who meant
the world
to them.

So I know
how you feel.

I know
what it is like
to wait
for someone all night,
while knowing
in the back of your head

they are not
going to come

home at all.

OUR TIME

We spend our time
chasing people

who aren't meant for us

and romanticizing

over things
that breaks us
in the most
beautiful of ways.

PEOPLE CHANGE

People change,

lovers become strangers,
and time goes on.

And most of the time,

it's the people
who hurt you the most

whom you never seem
to get over

at all.

TO FEEL NOTHING

Is it normal
to feel nothing at times?

It is normal
to wake up feeling
like a stranger
in your own body,

not knowing who you are
or who you want to be?

And I'm not sure
if I'm sad
or depressed
or just someone who has been
fucked over so many times
that I've forgotten who
I'm supposed to be.

My body has become
a vessel of pain,
of abandonment,

of all the things
that keep the numbing close
to my heart.

Maybe I'm asking

the wrong questions,
and I'm not trying
to be dramatic.
I never have.

It's just that sometimes
when I'm with her,
I feel different
and I notice these things,
and I notice other things
when she's not around.

Maybe I don't know
what I'm supposed to do
or who I'm supposed to be,
but none of that matters
when she's with me.

She makes me feel free.

She makes me feel alive,
and I know that's a cliché
but I don't care.

It's the truth.

I love her
for everything
she makes me feel
and more.

CONSIST OF

And sometimes
when we have a chance,
we don't take it.
And it is only
when the moment
is lost
that we appreciate it.

And this is what
our lives consist of:

the choices we make,
the people we miss,

and

the moments
we're meant to lose
forever.

SOMEONE TO BE THERE

I don't need
a savior.
I never did.

What I need
is someone to be there
for me
when I don't have enough
in me
to keep going.

Someone who respects me
and treats me well.

And someone
who doesn't go back
on their word

when they have promised
to be there,

no matter what.

PRETEND IT IS GOOD

Sometimes
you've got to pretend
that everything is going great
even when it's not.

That's what real hope
is like.

JOKES TO LAUGH

We can tell
each other jokes
that only we find funny.

We can stay up late
and not have to go to sleep
till morning.

We can have bad habits,
good habits,
it doesn't matter.

We can be birds
and fly toward the moon,
or we can rush toward the sky
and make it ours.

We can build our own world
out of nothing,

never come out of it,
and believe that there are
still

some places
worth fighting for.

I WENT TOO FAR

And yes,
maybe I went too far.

Maybe I pushed us
off the edge,
but that's how it works.

When you care about someone,
you go out
and beyond.

You push your limits
and theirs,
and in the end,

you come back stronger,
different,
and all that matters
is that

you kept going.

KINDER, STRONGER

Most people
are better
than they know:

stronger, kinder.

It's just that sometimes
they need someone
to remind them
of all the things

their hearts deserve.

FORGOTTEN PAIN

Despite the pain
others have caused,
you have got to
believe
that you have made
the right choices.

That you have left
people behind
because you had to
and not because you
wanted to.

That the things
you have felt
could have meant
anything.

And that you are more
in control of your life

than you know.

WHERE IT RAINS

This is where it is safe.

Where the walls
are covered in flames
and nothing can harm you.

Where hard days come later
rather than sooner
and the love I have for you
can be inhaled.

Where people come and go.

And where the darkness
consumes the light and
the light burns through
the darkness.

This is my heart
and these are my scars
and people always leave
and sometimes

I cannot help
but wonder why.

THE SOFTEST PART

The hardest part
of moving on
is thinking about
the other person:

wondering what their day
is like
and what goes through
their mind

as time goes on.

THAT DAY

Everyone has *that* day.

The day you realize
what you deserve
and what you don't.

And when that day
arrives,
everything changes.

You're okay
with letting things happen
the way they were
meant to happen
because when it's over,

all that matters
is how much you loved
and how much love

was given back to you
in return.

EMOTIONAL PERSON

And I can't change
the way I am,

for I'm an emotional person.
I question,
I reason,
and I feel.

And I'm learning this
little by little.

I'm learning that sometimes
my heart changes
faster than my mind,
and that my mind
doesn't always know
what's right,
what to do.

I'm learning that
my mistakes
are things I have to accept
and that the people
I can't have,
I must learn to let go of.

I'm learning,
and I'm okay

with not knowing everything.

I'm okay
with being myself,

no matter how many times
I fall.

PAIN MAN

Sometimes,

we spend our lives
chasing the people
who hurt us the hardest,

the deepest,

despite all the pain
they have caused.

TAKE YOU BACK

And I know
your heart aches.

And I know
people have broken you
but you can't take
all of that pain
to break someone back.

You can't hurt someone
because they've hurt you
first.

That's not how it works.

You break and you heal.

You forgive and you forget.

And then
your heart comes back

even stronger
than before.

STORMS CHASING

And of all
these storms,

it is the one
that keeps following me

that makes
the sound of your name.

LITTLE HARDER

And when we look back,

it is the days we remember
that define us.

The ones that took
our breath away
and the ones that
inspired us
to love

a little harder.

TO BE FELT

And now
look what you have
done.

You have got me here
smiling.

Feeling
all the feels
the way they were meant
to be felt.

You've got me
exploding,
expanding within myself.

And I think I'm doomed.

I think I'm in love
and I know

that everyone deserves this.

PARADISE

It is,
after all,

my pleasure
to find out more
about you

as time goes on

because
I know that within you,
within your heart,

there is a paradise
most men
are too afraid

to explore.

NO PLACES

Because happiness
is not a place
nor a destination.

Happiness
is a state of mind
and I don't need
a map to point me
in the right direction.

I have you,
in front of me,
and that's good enough
for me.

STRONGER LIFE

You can't give up
because bad things
happen to good people.

That's how it is.

Life goes to shit
sometimes, and it doesn't
matter what you've done.

Shit happens.

People leave,
they get lost,
and sometimes they never
find their way back home.

But you can't throw it all
away because of that.

You've come a long way.
You're better,
stronger,
and you just have to accept
that life just isn't fair
sometimes.

That is all.

WORTH IT

You know,
it's a curse when you
miss someone
but it's also
a blessing

because it means

you have someone
worth remembering.

NO SHAME

There's no shame
in being vulnerable.

Hell, we're all vulnerable
sometimes.

I'd be more concerned if you weren't,
because that means
you've got nothing worth breaking.

Nothing worth fixing,
healing, protecting,
and the heart needs to break
sometimes, you know?

It needs to be out of your chest.

It needs to be handled carelessly
at times.

How else are you going to know
what you're made of?

You've got to let it drop
 a few times before finding
the right person to hand it off to forever.

And sometimes

you don't find that person,
but who are we to stop trying?

To stop giving ourselves
to people we love,
to people we think
we love?

We have to hope for the best, right?
We've got to enter
other people's lives in hopes
that they'll be the ones
who inspire us to stay.

Nonetheless,
getting your heart broken
a few times isn't such a bad thing.
No one finds a lover
and tells them,

"Hey, you've got too many scars
within you, therefore
I can't love you."

No, actually it's quite the opposite.

The more lovers you have,
the better you'd be at giving love,
at recognizing it.

A lover finds another lover

and it's like a spell,
a chain of feelings,
a roller coaster of love.

That's why you have some people
who feel like they give more
of themselves—than others.

Because they've loved more
and have been broken
even harder.

RESPECT YOURSELF

You've got to respect yourself,
love yourself enough
to walk away from someone
who does you wrong.

Believe me,
it takes guts
cutting off someone
who doesn't serve you right,

and it's not such an awful thing
because it just means
you're finally realizing

that the only person
you should be holding on to

is yourself.

VALUABLE

You've got to take
what's in front of you

whether it's bad or good

because life is uncertain
and our greatest loss
will be not doing anything.

So you've got to understand
that choices are gold

and our actions

are more valuable
than you know.

BENEATH THE SEA

There are waves
inside of her
and sometimes
her past washes up
toward the shore,

and with faraway eyes
she cannot help
but wonder what has become
of all the people
she has let go of.

Of all the best parts
of herself,
the ones she has buried
beneath her sea.

She has more within her
then I'll ever know

and I'm ok with sharing my time
with her
as times goes on.

That's all.

ANOTHER IS BORN

She gives her best parts
to people
and still,
when she has nothing left,

she finds it within her
to give more.

She is a collection of stars,
and when one dies,
another is born.

She is all galaxy,
and has the color of
a tragic love
engraved on her bones.

HUMAN SURVIVAL

People are attracted
to strong people.

People with dreams
and aspirations.

People with confidence
and compassion.

People who are made of fire
and determination,
with the will to build,
not destroy.

Human survival
is based on these things
and love is possibly

the only feeling
that can make us believe
in all those things

again.

DARKEST HOURS

Perhaps
they do love you
but they don't show it enough.

And that's the saddest truth,
that you want it to feel real,
although,
you know it isn't…

because your heart keeps leading you
toward the wrong places.

And that's why you keep finding
the wrong people,
feeling the wrong feelings.

You keep chasing stars
in the middle of the day
and you keep looking for sunlight
during the darkest hours
of the sky.

WHERE IT LEADS

You see,
that's the secret.
Most of us are pretending.

Pretending to know
what we want.

Pretending to know
who we are.

Pretending to know
how we feel.

So don't feel too bad
if you don't know where you're going

or

what you're supposed to be doing,
because most of us
are following the same path

and none of us
really know where it leads.

BOMBS

But you know
what is stronger than bombs?

Inspiring people.

That's the kind of thing
that's strong enough

to change the world.

FILLED WITH LIFE

You can't keep looking
for your past in everyone
you meet.

Not everyone is going
to hurt you
the way they did.

Not everyone is the same.

You shouldn't look for ghosts
in places
filled with so much life.

TIME GOES ON

It's okay to let go
if it's not what you
want anymore.

No one is going
to hold you accountable
for all the things
you no longer feel

because life is short
and you know what you deserve

and it's okay
to change your mind.

All things change
as time goes on.

FALLING OFF

The people I need
have a strange way
of coming into my life

and the people I want
have a strange way
of falling off.

God, your sense of humor
is terrible,

thank you for making my life
more confusing—than that

of what
it already is.

NO GREAT PAIN

There is no greater pain
than watching the one
you love move on.

You begin to think
you weren't good enough,
and you begin to wonder
if they're thinking of you
when you're not around.

Letting go is hard,
but living with memories
is even harder.

They can kill you every time
you shut your eyes.

LOVED AT ALL

The one who breaks you
and the one who heals you
are never the same person.

And still,
you commit to the one
who drops you the hardest
because that's what people do.

Because we would rather know
what it's like to fall,
despite everything
we have ever known about flying.

Because we would rather burn,
despite what they've told us
about fire.

We would rather love
and get hurt
than not have loved at all.

YOUR ARMS

There's nothing sadder
than two people
who are meant to be together,

living side by side

without knowing
each other's names,

and passing through their lives

wondering

what it could have been like
to rest
in each other's arms.

HEART FOREVER

And it doesn't matter
how much time has passed.

So it could be a week,
a month,
a year,
or it could even be
longer than that.

It's just hard looking back,
thinking what became
of the people you once loved.

That's the kind of wonder
that stays
within the human heart forever.

TAME US

I know life is hard.

I know that sometimes
you feel like giving up

on people and on yourself.

I know you have good days
and bad days,
but more bad than good,
or so it seems.

I know that every day
you question yourself:

What is this all for?
Am I making the right choices?
Am I supposed to be here now?

I know
you have more questions
than answers,
and most of the time
you don't even know
how to explain them.

I know,
life is hard.

I know,
but you have to keep going.

You have to rise above
the waters of your soul
and bloom,
no matter how hot
the fire is.

No matter how many arrows
you carry on your back.

The times are hard,
I know,
believe me.

But you're a goddamn warrior,
a soldier filled with both pain
and love.

And life, well,
life is just another beast
you were meant to tame
and there is no one better for the job

than you.

MY OWN SKIN

Because sometimes
the most beautiful things
are born out of what deeply hurts,

and I've gone through
enough nights not knowing
who I am.

Not knowing what it means
to be alive.

But I'm working on it.

I'm working on myself every day.
Inside and out.

I'm working on all my faults
and I'm trying to reach
for the moon.

I'm trying to be
my own star
and I'm trying to light
my own sky.

That's all.

FIRE ON ANYONE

There's always someone
out there who understands.

Someone who has been
burned harder or who has seen,
experienced tragic things.

Know that these people
are the most beautiful.

Know that these people
understand what it's like
to pull knives out of their backs.

Know that these people
drink to the chaos of life
and that they accept it
for what it is.

Know these people.

Find these people
and bloom.

Find these people
and share both the light
and the darkness together.
Build.

Grow.

Forget but never regret
what has almost killed you.

Know that people
like this walk the earth
barefoot,
naked, and vulnerable.

Know that you are
not alone,
and know that the people
who tell you that they're with you
usually do not understand
what you've gone through.

Know that the people
who *do* understand
never wish the fire upon anyone.

What I'm trying to say is,

sometimes when you heal others,
you also heal yourself.

SPECTATING

It must be hard
to feel as if you could have
done something,
but instead you sat
and watched on the sidelines.

It must be hard
knowing that you could have
done more to prevent
something from happening.

It must be hard falling asleep
when saving someone
is the only thing
in your heart.

It must be hard
thinking
and thinking
and thinking of the other
possibilities.
If only you had tried
a little harder.

It must be hard
to live with this weight
on your shoulders,
reminding you

of what you should have done.

It must be hard to stand,
to breathe,
to walk,

when the heaviness
from letting things be
passes through.

The windows are broken,
but you should never hand over
more stones,

because doing nothing
is something,

and there is nothing worse than that.

Bullying is cruel,
but spectating
is even crueler.

I WANT THE

I want to wake up
free from this pain.

I want the days to feel longer,
and the nights
to take my breath away.

I want to swim in the ocean
whenever I feel like flying,
and I want to rest over the earth
whenever my body is aching.

I want this stress out of my life,
out of my heart,
and I want fear to dissolve
as I exhale.

I want to live,
goddammit.
Is that too much
to ask?

I want every moment
to make me feel
as if my life is meant
for something,
as if every step I take
is one step closer

to paradise.

I want love,
but not just any.

I want the kind that will keep me
on my toes,
and the kind where only fools
rush in.

That hard love,
that rare love,
you know?

I want the world,
all of it, for what it is
and what it was,
and for what it could be.

I just want to feel something,
anything that will catapult me
toward better days,
toward days where I am free,
where I am able to kiss
the sky
and grab a few stars
to claim as my own.

I want peace.
I want happiness.
I want to be me.

And this is the realest shit
I have ever written,
and I just want to keep it real
with myself,
even if that means

losing everyone I love.

THIS IS SOMETHING

This is something
about self-love—

something they don't teach
in school.

Something that's very hard
to learn on your own.

This is something
about putting yourself first
because it's okay
to love yourself before anyone else.

This is something about doing
what's best for you,
no matter what people say, because
only you know what you deserve.

This is something about being real,
being real to who you are
and accepting things
as they come and change.

This is something about your mistakes,
about your flaws,
and about how beautiful it is
to get up

and try again.

This is something about being you,
about using your voice
when you're afraid.

About building enough courage
when you feel like standing up
to something you don't believe in,
something that's wrong.

This is about you,
and every day should be about you,
and that's something
you should always consider.

Because self-love
is one hell of a drug.
It makes you invincible,
and that kind of strength
has never looked good on anyone
other than you.

So please,
take the time to focus on yourself,
to love yourself
and remember to put yourself
back together
every time you fall apart.

ONE DAY

One day
you will look back at your past
and you will forgive yourself
for your mistakes,

and on that day
you will accept your scars
and you will love yourself
no matter what.

CREATE DAYS

It is best to create moments,
because moments last longer
than people.

And people,
well,
people suck,
and you, my love,
are made of the best memories
they can offer.

So take this with you
as you go into the world,
and remember
that change is a blessing.

It's okay to wake up different

every
single
day.

FIND A WAY TO FLY

I know what it's like
to be afraid to speak up and use
your mind.

To be afraid
without knowing
what it is you're afraid of
to begin with.

I know what it's like
to be sitting quietly
in the middle of a crowd,
thinking
how your life isn't good enough,
while everyone around you
is enjoying theirs.

I know what it's like
to listen to your peers
as they talk about their goals
and dreams,
and you cannot help but wonder
what it is you're doing
with your own life,

whether you've made the right choices
or decisions.

I know what it's like
to wake up hating yourself
for not doing more,
for knowing what you have to do
but just not doing it
for whatever reason it may be.

I know what it's like
to stand still
while the world keeps spinning
around you,
and you cannot help
but let go
because you're not strong enough
to hold on.

I know what it's like
every night,
every day,
and I know
it feels like shit,
but I can tell you
that things do get better.

That not all moments
are meant to be lost.

That everything that happens
is to prepare you
for your perfect glory.

Remember
that time heals everything,
and what time doesn't heal,
you have to heal yourself.

Remember
that nothing is permanent,
that everything
finds a way to move on

and so should you.

Better days are ahead.

Believe me,
everything is waiting for you
on the other side

of doubt.

A FLOWER DIED

A flower died in my hands
and I think a part of me died with it.

It didn't make a sound
as I ripped it from all it's ever known.

At first
I wasn't aware of what I was doing.

I just wanted to have it in my hands,
to feel it, up close and personal.

We shared a moment.

A flower died in my hands
and I think a part of me died with it.

It didn't cry for help or mercy.

It didn't flinch
or move as I held it closer
to my eyes.

I wanted to let it go
but I couldn't.

My fingers tangled between
its stem

and its life poured
as so did mine.

We shared a moment.

A flower died in my hands
and I think a part of me died with it.

The flower didn't do anything
as it took its last breath of life.

It slowly faded away,
the same way I slowly dissolved
the moment I touched it.

We shared a moment.

A flower died in my hands
and I think a part of me died with it.

Since then
I haven't been the same.

I haven't been able
to let people in.

I haven't let people love me,
for fear of watching myself slip away.

A flower died in my hands
and I think a part of me died with it.

I think a part of me fell on the ground.

I think a part of me
found itself back in the earth,
to bloom anew
with both pain and love.

With both death and life.
With both darkness and light.

I share a moment with you.

So take it with you.

A flower died in my hands yesterday,
and I think a part of me has died as well,

and I think a part of you
has just died too,
as the words enter through your eyes
and make their way through your skull.

In this moment,
we become flowers.

We become the last of our kind.

I guess
people
and flowers
have something in common.

We both die slowly,
alone,
and when we hurt,

we barely make a sound.

PUSHING YOU OFF

I'm sorry for pushing you away.
The thing is,
I've had some bad experiences.

I've had a lot of trouble
with trusting people
and letting them in.

I know
that says a lot about
who I am.

I know that running away
and suddenly closing myself
makes me look a little crazy.

I know that pretending
everything is okay
will eventually catch up to me,
and I know
that loving me
must be one of those things,
one of those hard—
impossible things.

I know it's difficult to understand.
Hell,
it's difficult for me

to explain,
but the truth is that
I'm afraid to let people stay awhile.

I'm afraid
of watching people go.

I'm afraid
of being alone.

I'm afraid.

And that's how things begin
to fall apart for me,
because I know it all starts
with me
and I'm trying to change.

I'm trying to be different.
I'm trying to find the sun
where the darkness dwells.

It's just hard to find someone
when everyone you meet
expects so much more.

I just want to be myself,
and I want the person I'm with
to love me

for who I am.

FUCK OFF

I don't need you
to remind me
of how perfect your life is,
because I know
you're okay.

I know that somewhere
out there,
you're living your life
as you once told me you would.

I know
you're discovering new places,
sharing good times
with new people,
and making lovers
out of new friends.

Hell, I know you're okay,
and I'm okay too.

And I didn't come here
for an apology,
a revelation,
or anything of that cloth.

No, I came here for me.
I came here to let go.

I came here to face you,
to look you in the eyes
and tell myself
that I'm better now,

that you didn't fuck me over
as you thought you did.

No, never that.

I came here to make peace
with my past
as I welcome my future.

I came here
to tell you
that it doesn't hurt anymore,
that it never did
to begin with
because I love myself.

I love myself
ten thousand times
over and over.

I love myself
with flawed thoughts
and a heart full of scars.

I love myself
beaten

and barely alive.

I love myself
for all of my mistakes
and all of the pain
that has made me
who I am.

I love myself,
and this is the strongest feeling
I've ever felt
in my entire life,

and there's nothing more
fulfilling than that.

Thank you,

now fuck off.

THE BETTER PERSON

"Be the better person.
Learn when it's time
to walk away.
Don't hold grudges.
Don't go to sleep
with a foul heart."

Of course,
it is easier said
than done,
but you've got to
give these things a try.

And I know
it sounds ridiculous.

I know you know
what you're supposed to do,
think, and feel.

Well, of course you know,
but you don't follow it,
and still,
you don't know why.

The thing is,
love,
I don't know why

you cause yourself
so much pain.

I don't know why
you cling to the things
that break you the most.

I guess
it must be a human thing,
because when we see danger,
we run toward it
as fast as we can.

We collide running toward the things
that hurt us,
and we don't give a damn
if we survive.

We don't give a damn
of the consequences.

Because pain is inevitable,
of course,
we all know this.

And still,
we have to find it within ourselves
to be kind
to the things that break us.

We have to grow in places

that hurt us
the most
and find wholeness

in all things
that shatter.

FEATHERS FLYING

I cannot recall
what it is
about you.

What it is
that keeps me close
enough.

But I believe
it is because you break me.

Because every action you do
pushes me a little deeper in.

Because every time
I'm alone
the wine overflows in me
and I cannot ignore
the sound of your name.

Because I do not want
to talk about it
but it's the only goddamn thing
on my mind.

Because I do not care
about a thing,
I love you

like it hurts
and I feel the burning pain
with every breath
I take.

I do not understand,
but what I feel
is a strange little game,

because the more you run,
the closer I feel.

And the closer I feel,
the harder it is for me
to reach you.

Sometimes
you push me further away,
and sadly,

it only makes me love you
even more.

DON'T YELL

Don't tell me
you don't care
when you're the one
chasing people

and don't tell me
your heart
is made of stone

when every time
someone holds it

their hands turn
to gold.

THE STRUGGLE OF LOVE

It's troublesome,
I know,
because no matter the outcome,

no matter
every possibility
I play out in my head,

none of them
end with you.

BROKEN PEOPLE

To find
someone broken
and be able
to make them
feel beautiful.

That alone
might be
the most fulfilling
thing to do

in the world.

EXTREME ACTS

And now
the days are far more
relentless than before,
and I understand you because of it.

Because most men
will tell you special,
silly little things to use your love.

Because most men
will do extreme acts
with half a heart
just to have you for the night.

Gone are the soft
and gentle days.

Gone are the days
when you know
where you stand.

But I don't blame you.

I don't blame you
for the scars on your back,
on your heart.

Because life is an endless path

filled with broken glass,
and sometimes
the wounds run deep.

And most men are full of pain
and confusion,
therefore,
I know how difficult it is
to separate the lions
from the wolves…

the real men
from the ones who don't know
your worth.

Damn,
these choices aren't easy,
and some days are harder
than others,
more grim than others,
and most of the time
it's really hard to know what to feel,

when every man around you
is full of shit
and there aren't enough stalls
to occupy them all.

The struggle is real
and love isn't rare.
It's just that most men

wouldn't know what to do with love
if it presented itself

at their front door.

WALK AGAIN

It's sad to know
that I'll have
the rest of my life
to live without you.

To visit places
our bodies
were never meant
to walk

together

again.

MOMENTS AWAY

Despite the perfect love
everyone is always looking for,

I want to settle
for something different,
something real.

I want to be torn apart.
I want to be broken down
like a puzzle waiting
to be solved.

I want to be understood,
to be emptied,
to be filled up all over again.

I want to wake up
to someone for the rest of my life,
and I want that person
to tell me I'm enough,
regardless of my past.

And although
I already know this,

I want that person
to convince me that my scars
are beautiful,

that my flaws
are what made them love me.

And I don't want perfection
or validation,
just someone who will treat me
like a fucking human being

and remind me
that true happiness

is

always just a few moments

away.

DAMN THING

I want to imagine
myself happy.

I want to see myself,
whether it's five or
ten years
from now, with you.

I want to imagine us,
together,
giving each other
our best parts

and not questioning

a damn thing.

TIME TO TIME

You make me
feel special.

Like a human being
on the verge

of something
beautiful.

TOO LATE

Too often,
we say
and don't do
enough

and most of the time
we don't know

what we've done
until
it's too late.

IT IS OKAY

It is okay
to distance
yourself from people.

It is a blessing
to listen
to your own voice

when no one is
around.

BROKEN PIECES

What a beautiful thing
it is to adapt.

To learn from your mistakes
and build a new world

of all your broken pieces.

WALKING WHERE

And I died twice
with you:

the first time
I laid eyes on you

and the last time
I saw you walk away.

WHAT IS IT?

I find it both
a curse
and a blessing
to change one's heart.

To wake up
and choose to do nothing

or wake up
and know that you
deserve more.

SADNESS IN ME

It is sad
when someone
leaves you,

but it is
even sadder

when someone
forgets you.

That kind of
hurting

never really
abandons you.

YOU LOVE YOU

Some things
in this world
should never be explained,

like the first time
someone touches your soul,

the moment you discover
your purpose,

and the last time
you kiss someone
you love.

SINGLE WORD

Silence,
at times,
is a very powerful thing.

You can isolate
yourself from everyone
you know

or you can make
everyone listen

without saying
a single word.

RAIN STORMS

Each person
feels pain
their own way
and every storm
is different,

and when they feel
the rain,
they change.

YOU CANNOT

You can't do that.

You can't just come
into someone's life,
make them care
about you,
and abandon them
a few months later.

That kind of suffering
leaves a mark on the soul,
and it leaves a question,

one that never
gets answered
as time goes on.

AS LONG AS IT STANDS

Just because the one
you want ignores you
doesn't mean
you have to ignore
everyone else.

There are other people
who want to understand you,
love you.

Don't close yourself
to the possibility that
anything is possible,

and don't forget that
you have the right
to change your heart—
at any given moment

as long as it stands
for something.

POWER NO ONE

No matter how many times
you've failed,
you can start again.

After all,
people are marvelous creatures.
They possess a power
no other animal has.

They have the ability
to change their lives
and move on,

no matter how much
pain
the world has caused.

DISCOURAGED TONIGHT

You've been feeling
discouraged lately.

I could see it in your eyes.
I could see the light
of hope getting dimmer
and dimmer.

I know
times are hard
and some may even say
that they are not
worth fighting for.

That bad things happen
because they're supposed to
happen
and that there's no way
around it.

In so many levels,
I could agree with that
because I've seen more rain
than sunshine.

I've felt more fire than water.
I've discovered more tragedies

than miracles,
more losses than gains.

I could relate
because I, too,
feel discouraged.

Because I, too,
feel as if everyone is out
to get me.

I feel isolated.
I feel lost.
I feel so confused
at times,
beaten
and exhausted.

Like when
I find something worthwhile
I lose it
before I could even
appreciate it.

Yeah, I get it,
and although
we're not the same,
I feel what you feel.

I see what you see
and because of that,

I understand you.
I could look you in the eyes
and tell you
it's going to be okay.

Because we've all been there,
it's just that some of us
have a better way
of burying what hurts
and others
have a better way of digging it out

and I've had enough
of myself
exposed to tell you
that life gets better,
that it must go on,

no matter how dark
the times get.

The show doesn't sleep
if it rains.

Hope is always
on the edge of the horizon.

HEART BROKEN

It is not such
a bad thing
to feel sadness
from time to time.

To cry.
To let go
of your body.

To surrender
to the darkness
of your soul.

It is okay to feel terrible.

It is okay
to shut down
and block everyone out,
at any given moment.

You are entitled to shatter,
to heal,
to look beyond
the obvious and grow.

After all,
there is nothing scarier

in the world
than trusting
a person who has never
had their heart broken

at all.

OUR LIVES ARE SMALL

And yes,

we may fall in love
with other people.

We may
find our way
and relive similar moments too
but what saddens me deeply is

that we may never
live the same moment twice.

We will never kiss
the same lips
and we will forever
go to bed
wondering

what has become
of our lives.

ME AND MYSELF

I do not know
if I should hate you
or thank you.

Hate you
for breaking me apart

or thank you
for helping me
appreciate myself

more than before.

SOME PEOPLE

Some people
are not meant
to be ours.

Some people
we have to let go
and watch them go

but the beauty of it all is,

that sometimes
they do come back.

Sometimes you do
get a second chance.

Sometimes history
does repeat itself,
and sometimes there are
happy endings.

That's the blessing of life:
things happen for a reason,

and when they do

sometimes
the outcome is beautiful.

WHO DID WHAT

They left for a reason,
so don't look back
and feel heartbreak.

The past doesn't have mercy
on the future
and sometimes
the future isn't shaped
by the past.

You design your own
destiny,
and you should never
build a home
out of those

who broke you.

WHAT YOU HAVE DONE

Some days,
you will feel broken
and you will feel
the layer of sadness
thicker than before.

But I will tell you
to live by this
and to know this
as if your life
depended on it.

Know that all things pass,

that all sadness heals,
and that all moments
are lived once,

no matter who you are,
and what you've done.

FUTURE STUFF

Don't expect
too much
from people

because you'll always
end up
disappointed

and don't overthink,
because
that's that type
of thing

that could destroy you.

DO NOT BEG

You shouldn't beg people
to stay,
and you shouldn't
beg for their attention either.

Because most people
are like boomerangs.

You can toss them
as far as you can,
and if the moment
is right,
they'll always come back
to where they started.

So it's okay
to be alone,
at least for now.

I guess
what I'm trying to say is,
that it's okay to give people space,
to give them time.

Soon enough
they'll find their way
back home.
All you have to do

is wait,
and make sure
you're there when you hear
a familiar knock

coming
from the front door.

LIFE FOREVER MAN

You go through life
meeting people,
so many
that you begin to lose track
of who is who.

You make friends,
you make lovers,
and then it all
goes away.

The heart grows in solitude.

Not many things change
but one thing is certain,
at night,

when everyone is gone
and you're alone
on your bed,
thinking,
that there is only one person
worth remembering,

You think.
You think.
You think.

That's who your heart
belongs to.

That's the person who's
meant to change your life
forever.

You go through life
meeting people,

but only one
will grant you life
until the sun
reaches its end.

WHAT I KNOW

I know you
want to let them know
that they didn't
break you,
but you don't have to prove
yourself to anyone.

You don't owe anyone anything.

They're wrong about you.

You're strong
and you don't break
that easily.

You're a goddamn rock
falling off a cliff.

Your heart is soft
but it is also ferocious enough
to end the world,

and that's
the only truth
you need to know.

ALWAYS BE HERE

Sometimes,
when it's over,
all you're left with is
regret
and the reality
of not taking the time
to say what you once
felt.

And that's what hurts
the most,
the fact that at some point
you had the opportunity

but you didn't take it
and you didn't
because you thought

the people you needed most
would always

be there.

TIME AND HEALING

You need space
to heal, time.

So it's okay
to get away.

It's okay
to travel across
the universe
without looking back.

It's okay to forget,
to close yourself up
and reevaluate
what you've done,
what you're meant
to do.

No one is going to destroy you
for distancing yourself.

No one is going to
hate you
for trying to make sense
of everything
and everyone
around you
because it's human.

It's the type of questioning
we must all go through

to discover

who we are.

BAD TRUTH

Everyone is always
telling you
who to be with.

"Be with someone
who loves you."

"Be with someone
who makes you happy."

"Be with someone
who brings out
the best in you."

How about
you be with someone
who understands you,
who feels
what you feel
and respects all walks
of life.

Someone who reveals
the truth
no matter how bad it is
and someone
who is not afraid
to hurt your feelings.

Be with someone,
anyone,
who makes you feel
at home
or don't be with anyone
at all.

No one should tell you
who is right for you.

After all,

that is something
you have to figure out
yourself.

MESSY LIFE

Life is supposed to be messy.

Can you imagine
how awful it would be
if it wasn't?

This would be a planet
filled with a bunch of
assholes
driving their perfect cars,
working their perfect jobs,
speaking about their perfect
lives.

Hell, imagine that.
Wouldn't that be a sight?
But thankfully it's not.

And besides,
I kind of love my crazy life.

I like waking up late,
I like rushing to work,
ending up in strange places
during strange times.

I like drinking
my average coffee

and sometimes,
I even like falling in love
with the wrong people.

Because despite everything,
it means I have so much more
to look forward to

and I know
that my hardest decision
will always be
who to spend my nights with
and with whom to share this laughter
I have trapped within me.

Because life is hard,
letting go is hard,

but loving the people
in your life
should be easy.

IMPORTANT ART

I don't want to teach you
how to love
or who to love
because that's something
that can't be taught.

I want to teach you
how to respect people's opinions,
people's art.

I want to teach you
how to appreciate something
ignored.

To see color
in a black-
and-white world.

I want to teach you
how to dream,

how to inspire people
to seek the truth
and to ignore the bullshit
the media feeds them.

I want to teach you
about expression,

acceptance,
and the power of self-love.

Because there are other things
that matter,

other things besides finding
someone to love.

Things that have to do
with morality,
with the way we treat
each other,
you know?

Things that bring people together
to build a generation
full of compassion.

That's what's important here.

TRAGIC LIFE

You don't get over people
by meeting new people.

That's not how it works.

Some people are not
replaceable,
and some people
come into our lives
to make us realize that.

But I get it:

a lot of things have affected you
and you're exhausted
by people,
all types too.

Especially the ones
close to you
and the ones you barely know.

I know what it's like,
that is,
to have this heavy feeling
in your gut,
the one that keeps telling you
to start over,

to pack your things
and leave it all behind.

We've all been there.

We've all been broken down
by people,
but that doesn't mean
you've got to give up
on them.

People are going
to let you down,
they're going to have
bad days,
a lot of them,
but the trick is
to find the ones
worth keeping
and to hold on to them

no matter how tragic
life gets.

CPSIA information can be obtained
at www.ICGtesting.com
Printed in the USA
BVOW03s1845071117
499786BV00001B/87/P